Project 1 :

Lucky Recipient:

Start Date:

Completion Deadline:

Project 2 :

Lucky Recipie.

Start Date:

Completion Deadline:

Project 3 :

Lucky Recipient:

Start Date:

Completion Deadline:

Project 4 :

Lucky Recipient:

Start Date:

Completion Deadline:

Project 5 :

Lucky Recipient:

Start Date:

Completion Deadline:

Project 6 :

Lucky Recipient:

Start Date:

Completion Deadline:

Project 7 :

Lucky Recipient:

Start Date:

Completion Deadline:

Project 8 :

Lucky Recipient:

Start Date:

Completion Deadline:

Project 9 :

Lucky Recipient:

Start Date:

Completion Deadline:

Project 10 :

Lucky Recipient:

Start Date:

Completion Deadline:

Project :

Start Date: _____   Completion Date: _____

Lucky Recipient: _____

Completion Deadline: _____

Occasion/Event: _____

Pattern Name: _____   Pattern #: _____

Pattern Designer: _____

Finished Quilt Size: _____

☐ Pieced   ☐ Applique   ☐ English Paper Pieced

Color Scheme: _____

Theme: _____

Story/Notes: _____

_____

_____

Thread Type/Weight: _____   Thread Color: _____

Stitch Number: _____   Stitch Style: _____

Stitch Length: _____   Stitch Width: _____

To Do List	Time Spent	Notes
☐ Plan Quilt		
☐ Select Fabric		
☐ Cut		
☐ Piece		
☐ Assemble		
☐ Back		
☐ Baste		
☐ Quilt		
☐ Bind		
☐ Brand		
TOTAL TIME:		

Materials List	Own	Buy	Retailer/Supplier
	☐	☐	
	☐	☐	
	☐	☐	
	☐	☐	
	☐	☐	
	☐	☐	
	☐	☐	

Colors & Fabric Swatches

Quick Quilt Plan

Layout Planning

Layout Planning

Completed Project Photos/Notes :

Completed Project Photos/Notes :

Project :

Start Date: Completion Date:

Lucky Recipient:

Completion Deadline:

Occasion/Event:

Pattern Name: Pattern #:

Pattern Designer:

Finished Quilt Size:

☐ Pieced   ☐ Applique   ☐ English Paper Pieced

Color Scheme:

Theme:

Story/Notes:

Thread Type/Weight: Thread Color:

Stitch Number: Stitch Style:

Stitch Length: Stitch Width:

To Do List	Time Spent	Notes
☐ Plan Quilt		
☐ Select Fabric		
☐ Cut		
☐ Piece		
☐ Assemble		
☐ Back		
☐ Baste		
☐ Quilt		
☐ Bind		
☐ Brand		
TOTAL TIME:		

Materials List	Own	Buy	Retailer/Supplier
	☐	☐	
	☐	☐	
	☐	☐	
	☐	☐	
	☐	☐	
	☐	☐	
	☐	☐	

Colors & Fabric Swatches

Quick Quilt Plan

Layout Planning

Layout Planning

Completed Project Photos/Notes :

Completed Project Photos/Notes :

Project :

Start Date: .... Completion Date: ....

Lucky Recipient: ....

Completion Deadline: ....

Occasion/Event: ....

Pattern Name: .... Pattern #: ....

Pattern Designer: ....

Finished Quilt Size: ....

☐ Pieced ☐ Applique ☐ English Paper Pieced

Color Scheme: ....

Theme: ....

Story/Notes: ....

Thread Type/Weight: .... Thread Color: ....

Stitch Number: .... Stitch Style: ....

Stitch Length: .... Stitch Width: ....

To Do List	Time Spent	Notes
☐ Plan Quilt		
☐ Select Fabric		
☐ Cut		
☐ Piece		
☐ Assemble		
☐ Back		
☐ Baste		
☐ Quilt		
☐ Bind		
☐ Brand		
TOTAL TIME:		

Materials List	Own	Buy	Retailer/Supplier
	☐	☐	
	☐	☐	
	☐	☐	
	☐	☐	
	☐	☐	
	☐	☐	
	☐	☐	

Colors & Fabric Swatches

Quick Quilt Plan

Layout Planning

Layout Planning

Completed Project Photos/Notes :

Completed Project Photos/Notes :

Project :

Start Date: Completion Date:

Lucky Recipient:

Completion Deadline:

Occasion/Event:

Pattern Name: Pattern #:

Pattern Designer:

Finished Quilt Size:

☐ Pieced   ☐ Applique   ☐ English Paper Pieced

Color Scheme:

Theme:

Story/Notes:

Thread Type/Weight: Thread Color:

Stitch Number   Stitch Style:

Stitch Length: Stitch Width:

To Do List	Time Spent	Notes
☐ Plan Quilt		
☐ Select Fabric		
☐ Cut		
☐ Piece		
☐ Assemble		
☐ Back		
☐ Baste		
☐ Quilt		
☐ Bind		
☐ Brand		
TOTAL TIME:		

Materials List	Own	Buy	Retailer/Supplier
	☐	☐	
	☐	☐	
	☐	☐	
	☐	☐	
	☐	☐	
	☐	☐	
	☐	☐	

Colors & Fabric Swatches

Quick Quilt Plan

Layout Planning

Layout Planning

Completed Project Photos/Notes :

Completed Project Photos/Notes :

Project :

Start Date: _____ Completion Date: _____

Lucky Recipient: _____

Completion Deadline: _____

Occasion/Event: _____

Pattern Name: _____ Pattern #: _____

Pattern Designer: _____

Finished Quilt Size: _____

☐ Pieced   ☐ Applique   ☐ English Paper Pieced

Color Scheme: _____

Theme: _____

Story/Notes: _____

_____

_____

_____

_____

Thread Type/Weight: _____ Thread Color: _____

Stitch Number: _____ Stitch Style: _____

Stitch Length: _____ Stitch Width: _____

To Do List	Time Spent	Notes
☐ Plan Quilt		
☐ Select Fabric		
☐ Cut		
☐ Piece		
☐ Assemble		
☐ Back		
☐ Baste		
☐ Quilt		
☐ Bind		
☐ Brand		
TOTAL TIME:		

Materials List	Own	Buy	Retailer/Supplier
	☐	☐	
	☐	☐	
	☐	☐	
	☐	☐	
	☐	☐	
	☐	☐	
	☐	☐	

Colors & Fabric Swatches

Quick Quilt Plan

Layout Planning

Layout Planning

Completed Project Photos/Notes :

Completed Project Photos/Notes :

Project :

Start Date: _____ Completion Date: _____

Lucky Recipient: _____

Completion Deadline: _____

Occasion/Event: _____

Pattern Name: _____ Pattern #: _____

Pattern Designer: _____

Finished Quilt Size: _____

☐ Pieced ☐ Applique ☐ English Paper Pieced

Color Scheme: _____

Theme: _____

Story/Notes: _____

_____

_____

_____

Thread Type/Weight: _____ Thread Color: _____

Stitch Number: _____ Stitch Style: _____

Stitch Length: _____ Stitch Width: _____

To Do List	Time Spent	Notes
☐ Plan Quilt		
☐ Select Fabric		
☐ Cut		
☐ Piece		
☐ Assemble		
☐ Back		
☐ Baste		
☐ Quilt		
☐ Bind		
☐ Brand		
TOTAL TIME:		

Materials List	Own	Buy	Retailer/Supplier
	☐	☐	
	☐	☐	
	☐	☐	
	☐	☐	
	☐	☐	
	☐	☐	
	☐	☐	

Colors & Fabric Swatches

Quick Quilt Plan

Layout Planning

Layout Planning

Completed Project Photos/Notes :

Completed Project Photos/Notes :

Project :

Start Date: Completion Date:

Lucky Recipient:

Completion Deadline:

Occasion/Event:

Pattern Name: Pattern #:

Pattern Designer:

Finished Quilt Size:

☐ Pieced   ☐ Applique   ☐ English Paper Pieced

Color Scheme:

Theme:

Story/Notes:

Thread Type/Weight: Thread Color:

Stitch Number: Stitch Style:

Stitch Length: Stitch Width:

To Do List	Time Spent	Notes
☐ Plan Quilt		
☐ Select Fabric		
☐ Cut		
☐ Piece		
☐ Assemble		
☐ Back		
☐ Baste		
☐ Quilt		
☐ Bind		
☐ Brand		
TOTAL TIME:		

Materials List	Own	Buy	Retailer/Supplier
	☐	☐	
	☐	☐	
	☐	☐	
	☐	☐	
	☐	☐	
	☐	☐	
	☐	☐	

Colors & Fabric Swatches

Quick Quilt Plan

Layout Planning

Layout Planning

Project :

Start Date: Completion Date:

Lucky Recipient:

Completion Deadline:

Occasion/Event:

Pattern Name: Pattern #:

Pattern Designer:

Finished Quilt Size:

☐ Pieced   ☐ Applique   ☐ English Paper Pieced

Color Scheme:

Theme:

Story/Notes:

Thread Type/Weight: Thread Color:

Stitch Number   Stitch Style:

Stitch Length: Stitch Width:

To Do List	Time Spent	Notes
☐ Plan Quilt		
☐ Select Fabric		
☐ Cut		
☐ Piece		
☐ Assemble		
☐ Back		
☐ Baste		
☐ Quilt		
☐ Bind		
☐ Brand		
TOTAL TIME:		

Materials List	Own	Buy	Retailer/Supplier
	☐	☐	
	☐	☐	
	☐	☐	
	☐	☐	
	☐	☐	
	☐	☐	
	☐	☐	

Colors & Fabric Swatches

Quick Quilt Plan

Layout Planning

Layout Planning

Completed Project Photos/Notes :

Completed Project Photos/Notes :

Project :

Start Date: _____ Completion Date: _____

Lucky Recipient: _____

Completion Deadline: _____

Occasion/Event: _____

Pattern Name: _____ Pattern #: _____

Pattern Designer: _____

Finished Quilt Size: _____

☐ Pieced ☐ Applique ☐ English Paper Pieced

Color Scheme: _____

Theme: _____

Story/Notes: _____

_____

_____

Thread Type/Weight: _____ Thread Color: _____

Stitch Number: _____ Stitch Style: _____

Stitch Length: _____ Stitch Width: _____

To Do List	Time Spent	Notes
☐ Plan Quilt		
☐ Select Fabric		
☐ Cut		
☐ Piece		
☐ Assemble		
☐ Back		
☐ Baste		
☐ Quilt		
☐ Bind		
☐ Brand		
TOTAL TIME:		

Materials List	Own	Buy	Retailer/Supplier
	☐	☐	
	☐	☐	
	☐	☐	
	☐	☐	
	☐	☐	
	☐	☐	
	☐	☐	

Colors & Fabric Swatches

Quick Quilt Plan

Layout Planning

Layout Planning

Completed Project Photos/Notes :

Completed Project Photos/Notes :

Project :

Start Date: Completion Date:

Lucky Recipient:

Completion Deadline:

Occasion/Event:

Pattern Name: Pattern #:

Pattern Designer:

Finished Quilt Size:

☐ Pieced   ☐ Applique   ☐ English Paper Pieced

Color Scheme:

Theme:

Story/Notes:

Thread Type/Weight: Thread Color:

Stitch Number: Stitch Style:

Stitch Length: Stitch Width:

To Do List	Time Spent	Notes
☐ Plan Quilt		
☐ Select Fabric		
☐ Cut		
☐ Piece		
☐ Assemble		
☐ Back		
☐ Baste		
☐ Quilt		
☐ Bind		
☐ Brand		
TOTAL TIME:		

Materials List	Own	Buy	Retailer/Supplier
	☐	☐	
	☐	☐	
	☐	☐	
	☐	☐	
	☐	☐	
	☐	☐	
	☐	☐	

Colors & Fabric Swatches

Quick Quilt Plan

Layout Planning

Layout Planning

Completed Project Photos/Notes :

Completed Project Photos/Notes :

Precut Fabric Measurements

Fat Quarter	18" x 21"
Fat Eighth	9" x 21"
Charm Packs	5" x 5"
Mini Charms	2.5" x 2.5"
Honey Buns	1.5" x 44"* Strips
Jelly Roll	2.5" x 44"* Strips
Dessert Roll	5" x 44"* Strips
Jolly Bar	5" x 10"
Layer Cake	10" Squares
Turnover	6" Triangles (x2 = 5" square)
Honeycomb	6" Hexagons

Yardage Measurements

1/8 Yard	4.5" x 44"*
1/4 Yard	9" x 44"*
1/3 Yard	12" x 44"*
1/2 Yard	18" x 44"*
2/3 Yard	24" x 44"*
3/4 Yard	27" x 44"*
One Yard	36" x 44"*

* OR WIDTH OF FABRIC

Common Quilt Sizes

Baby / Crib Quilt
36" x 60"

Twin Quilt
70" x 90"

Double/Full Quilt
84" x 108"

Queen Quilt
90" x 108"

King Quilt
110" x 108"

California King Quilt
106" x 112"

Made in the USA
Monee, IL
09 September 2021